A FAIR COUNTRY

A FAIR COUNTRY

Jon Robin Baitz

THEATRE COMMUNICATIONS GROUP

ISBN 1–56865–379–4

Cover art by James McMullan
Cover design by Donna Moy
Text design and composition by Lisa Govan

Printed in the United States of America

For Dan S.

A FAIR COUNTRY

A Fair Country opened at Lincoln Center Theater's Mitzi E. Newhouse Theater in New York City on February 19, 1996. The sets were designed by Tony Walton, the lights by James F. Ingalls, the costumes by Jane Greenwood, the sound by Scott Lehrer and original music was composed by Robert Waldman. Daniel Sullivan directed the following cast:

GIL BURGESS	Matt McGrath
PATRICE BURGESS	Judith Ivey
HILTON	Teagle F. Bougere
TOGO POLICEMAN	Maduka Steady
HARRY BURGESS	Laurence Luckinbill
ELLSWORTH HODGES	Jack Davidson
VICTOR	Maduka Steady
ALEC BURGESS	Dan Futterman
GERRIT VAN EDEN	Richard Clarke
CARLY FLETCHER	Katie Finneran

A Fair Country was workshopped at Seattle Repertory Theatre during their 1994–95 New Play Workshop Series in April 1995. Sets were by Thomas Gregg Meyer, lights by Jay Strevey, costumes by Catherine Meacham Hunt and sound by David Pascal. Daniel Sullivan directed the following cast:

GIL BURGESS	Neil Patrick Harris
PATRICE BURGESS	Joyce Van Patten
ELLSWORTH HODGES/HILTON	Peter Jay Fernandez
HARRY BURGESS	James Naughton
ALEC BURGESS	T. Scott Cunningham
GERRIT VAN EDEN	Kurt Beattie
CARLY FLETCHER	Ann Buchanan

A Fair Country received a workshop production at New York City's Naked Angels in November 1994. Set design was by Adrianne Lobel, lights by Brian MacDevitt, costumes by Jane Greenwood, sound by John Kilgore and original music was composed by Rick Baitz. David Warren directed the following cast:

GIL BURGESS	Matt McGrath
PATRICE BURGESS	Maria Tucci
ELLSWORTH HODGES/GERRIT VAN EDEN	Herb Foster
HARRY BURGESS	Ron Rifkin
ALEC BURGESS	Patrick Breen
CARLY FLETCHER	Mary McCormack

The play was presented as a workshop by New York Stage and Film and the Powerhouse Theater at Vassar College in July 1994. David Warren directed the following cast:

GIL BURGESS	Justin Kirk
PATRICE BURGESS	Maria Tucci
ELLSWORTH HODGES/GERRIT VAN EDEN	Keith Charles
HARRY BURGESS	Ron Rifkin
ALEC BURGESS	Patrick Breen
CARLY FLETCHER	Nadia Dajani

The playwright would like to thank John Patrick Shanley for encouraging him to pick up the abandoned shards of a broken play and keep going forward.

Characters

Gil Burgess   Harry Burgess   Gerrit Van Eden
Patrice Burgess   Togolese   Carly Fletcher
Hilton   Policeman   Announcer
Ellsworth Hodges   Allie Burgess

Time and Place

ACT ONE

Scene 1   1987. An archaeological excavation site in
            southern Mexico.

Scene 2   1977. Veranda of the Burgess home in Durban,
            South Africa.

Scene 3   The same day. Togo Airport, West Africa.

Scene 4   The next morning. Veranda of the Burgess home.

ACT TWO

Scene 1   1980. The Hague, Holland. The Burgess
            living room.

Scene 2   A few hours later.

Scene 3   1987. The excavation site.

Say this city has ten million souls,
Some are living in mansions, some are living in holes:
Yet there's no place for us, my dear, yet there's
     no place for us.

Once we had a country and we thought it fair,
Look in the atlas and you'll find it there:
We cannot go there now, my dear, we cannot go there now.

In the village churchyard there grows an old yew,
Every spring it blossoms anew:
Old passports can't do that, my dear, old passports
     can't do that.

The consul banged the table and said:
"If you've got no passport you're officially dead":
But we are still alive, my dear, but we are still alive.

                              —from "Refugee Blues"
                              by W. H. Auden

" ACT ONE "

Scene 1

Southern Mexico, 1987

A clearing in the jungle. A remote archaeological dig near the Guatemalan border. There is perhaps only a tent. A hint of jungle on all sides.

    Gil Burgess, a young man in dust-covered shorts and T-shirt is working with a brush and tweezers at the excavation site, carefully examining the shards of an ancient Mayan pot. He does not notice that he is being watched by a middle-aged woman, in sensible traveling clothes, who has appeared at the clearing. She silently studies him for a long moment before speaking.

PATRICE: Hello, Gil.

GIL *(Startled, he shakes his head, and laughs)*: I'm hallucinating. Right?

PATRICE: No.

GIL: It's what happens when you're alone.

PATRICE: It's really actually, *me.*

GIL *(Completely stunned)*: Oh, Christ.

PATRICE *(Studying him from the other side of the clearing)*: You look so different.

GIL: Do I? Huh.

(Beat) You tracked me down. Mother.

(He laughs) What did you do? Did you think that would be a good thing? That I would be—

(Beat) You heard yourself speaking to me? My response? I'm curious because . . .

PATRICE: Oh, I've had this exact conversation several times, in my head. Believe me.

GIL: And how did it end?

PATRICE: I never actually got that far.

GIL: You know, *nobody* ever finds me. I get *no* mail. No *news*. But *you*, Patrice, somehow, manage to track me down. Here!

(Beat) Amazing.

PATRICE *(A small shrug)*: Mothers. We do these things. A skill.

(Beat) An awful place, this. So isolated and that jungle . . . *(Still not moving, both are very wary)*

GIL: I sort of have become kind of fond of it.

(Beat, a small smile) You know. Home. Such as it is. I like it here. There are absolutely zero distractions.

(There is some sort of moment between them. A private connection.)

PATRICE *(Taking in the camp)*: You're looking for the great lost Mayan city?

GIL: It was a mistake, you know, your coming here. Whatever you thought. Whatever *transaction* you imagined.

PATRICE: Yes. But may I have some water?

GIL *(Sighs, hands her a canteen)*: We have a well. It tastes a little like egg salad and iodine. Do you take betaine hydrochloride? You'll get sick if you don't. You'll get sick anyway.

(*A shrug*) It's Mexico.

PATRICE *(Drinking)*: I'm somehow resistant.

GIL *(Can't help but smile)*: The microbes know better than to mess with you.

PATRICE: I don't know why. I ate on the train. At the little stands on the streets in San Cristobal. Americans around me dropping like flies.

GIL *(Shrugs)*: You're a survivor.

(*Pause*) How did you actually get out here?

PATRICE: Some farmer. A truck.

GIL: Indian or white?

PATRICE: Indian.

GIL: And you just got in his truck?

PATRICE: You're too thin, Gil.

GIL *(Surprised)*: I'm too thin? Am I?

(*Beat*) Huh.

PATRICE: Harry died.

GIL: Oh. Well. No. I understand this trip then. You wanted to tell me . . .

PATRICE: I'm so sorry to blurt it out. It's better that way.

GIL: Is it? Better? "Hi. Been a while. Love Mexico. Your dad is dead. May I have some *water*?"

(*Beat*) How did he die?

PATRICE: *Not well.*

GIL *(This is hilarious to him)*: "Not well"? What does that mean?

PATRICE: Cancer.

GIL *(Not a surprise)*: Well, I mean, all that red meat. The cigars. The boredom. You know these men lead these lives and—

PATRICE: He was trying homeopathic . . .

GIL: Was he? God. I can't picture . . . *(Gil cringes at the thought)* I don't think I want the details. Mom.

PATRICE: Well, they're not so pretty. I don't blame you.

(They stare at each other. Then Gil laughs—a bitter little snort.)

GIL *(Softening)*: How are things back in the States?

PATRICE: Reagan, it seems, has been selling Coke and guns from the Oval Office.

    (Beat) A disappointment.

GIL: So now that you've delivered your news, been the messenger, and all, you can go back to Santa Barbara. Mission accomplished and all.

PATRICE: I moved. Washington D.C. Georgetown.

GIL *(Genuinely surprised)*: Oh.

    (Beat) I have to say: A letter. It would have been sort of fine. I could have read it. At my own pace. News of the world.

PATRICE: No limit, is there, to the half-life of the anger of one's children.

GIL: One's *child*, Patrice. There's only one left. Just me.

PATRICE: Look. Gil. I didn't see a single other truck or vehicle of any sort along this road. It's not well traveled. I can't just walk out of this place.

GIL: No.

PATRICE: For God's sake. It's been six years. I mean— *(She stops. There is a silence)*

GIL *(Quietly)*: And are you still crazy, Mom?

PATRICE *(Grinning)*: Let's not stand on ceremony, shall we? They have all sorts of miracles, the mental health professionals. They have it all sorted out.

GIL *(A tiny smile)*: Finally.

(They look at each other for a moment, both smiling, a kind of easy enjoyment slips in.)

PATRICE: But you're here all alone?

GIL: The team's in Mexico City. The government wants to build a dam on this spot. So we'd be about forty feet underwater here. We're trying to get them to hold off a little longer.

PATRICE: I meant—*you're alone.*

GIL: My *boyfriend* went back to London. To his girlfriend. In Camden Town. Where they've got running water and MTV.

PATRICE: I'm sorry to hear that.

GIL: It's okay. I used to warn all my boyfriends that I was on the rebound from you.

PATRICE *(Enjoying him)*: Yes. Indeed.

GIL: Sit. I mean, if you want. I have to keep working at this.

(Gil goes back to the excavation. He looks into the pit and kneels beside the pottery shards.)

PATRICE: What is it?

GIL *(Looks up at her, a small smile)*: Broken pots. Ceremonial. Pottery. A cup. Perhaps used for the collection of blood.

After a sacrifice or two. You know, the Mayans, they're supposed to be the civilized ones, but all these ancient people down here, they all loved a little blood sport.

(He hands a piece of pottery to her) Here. Look.

PATRICE: An important find?

GIL: A hopeful one. We had made promises to the Mexican government. Slightly too enthusiastic, I thought, but you know, I'm too cautious, they tell me. We had claimed this as the site of an "important" Mayan settlement with its own gods and symbols. But nothing. Until this.

(Beat) I think this pot shard—if there's more, if I can find the *whole thing*—it might get us another year.

PATRICE *(Looking around her, a sigh)*: Cause for celebration. It's like that joke. "First prize—a week in Durban. Second prize . . ."

GIL *(Nodding)*: "Two weeks." Exactly.

(Beat. He looks at the shard of pottery in his hand) Yes. If I can hold on to it. We have looters. I mean, I don't know, here. By myself. They waited until the others were gone, and it was just me. It's big business down here. I saw him. My looter. A sort of slightly starving looking little guy with torn huaraches and wasted muscles. I chased him away. You have to show you're not scared. That you're in fact—*macho*. You can imagine how well I do.

PATRICE: But you do get scared?

GIL *(A rush)*: They've been gone two whole weeks! I mean, what are they *doing*? Sitting in some bar in Mexico City, in air conditioning, you know? How long does it take to get dismissed by an assistant secretary at the Ministry of Archaeological Fuckups? I can't even get word to them that in fact I've found something . . . I . . . just wait. Dig.

PATRICE: Sunset.

(They look at the diminishing daylight.)

PATRICE *(Remembering)*: We used to go camping. Do you recall that? You were too young probably. The four of us. Very intrepid. Very . . . wonderful.

GIL: Once in Montauk. Once in Big Sur. Yosemite. Somewhere between Cape Town and Port Elizabeth on the beach.

PATRICE: And we would tell stories?

GIL: Yes. Well. We were a family, that's what families do. But now— No way. Listen.

    (Beat, a quiet rage) I don't want to tell stories. It doesn't do—

    (Beat) Look. Sometimes there's a truck at first light. Heading to the border.

    (Beat. He looks at his watch) Nine hours.

(A moment, Gil's vehemence shocks her.)

PATRICE *(Then softly)*: Nine hours. Okay. We have nine hours.

(The lights fade on the two of them.)

Scene 2

Durban, December 1977

The veranda of a Cape-Dutch house on the North Coast of Natal. It is late afternoon. The remains of a shattered Zulu pot are on the steps and the ground. A black gardener, Hilton, enters carrying a bag filled with women's clothes.

GIL *(Entering)*: Hilton! Her stuff! They're waiting for her stuff!

(The sounds of a car pulling away. Gil, surprised, looks after it.)

They *left.*

HILTON: The Durban police don't wait. They're very busy.

GIL: But how's she gonna . . . ? *(Gil holds out the bag toward Hilton)* Can you get this down to her?

HILTON *(Gruff)*: They have clothes for her in jail.

GIL: Jesus, Hilton! What happened? Did she just go berserk all of a sudden?

HILTON: I didn't see. I heard her screaming, and I came when you did.

GIL: But *why* was she *screaming*?

(Patrice enters and sees the broken pot.)

PATRICE: Oh, great. She got this one too.

(Beat.)

GIL: They just drove off. I couldn't even give them her stuff.

(He gently kicks the bag of clothes. A moment.)

PATRICE *(Takes this in)*: Hilton, what I need for you to do right now is make us some tea. Would you mind taking over the kitchen? Just for right now, would you mind?

HILTON: *(Very obsequiously)*: Of course . . . Do you want fancy tea or teabag tea?

PATRICE *(Impatiently)*: Just *tea*.

(Hilton exits.)

GIL *(Fretting)*: Should I call someone from the consulate, Mom?

PATRICE: Christ, *no*. That's all your father would need.
     (Beat. Annoyed) Please don't hover like some mendicant. Everything is okay. It's really fine. Let's just get this all picked up. *(Taking in the broken pottery)* Maybe your father can piece this together when he gets back. His next big cultural project!

GIL: I just wish the whole business were a bit clearer.

PATRICE: Are you still shaken up?

GIL: I don't understand what set her off.

PATRICE: The thing is, she and I had a little run in. I may have forgotten the rules for a second. I may have forgotten that she is the maid and I am the mistress. *Role* confusion.

GIL: But she was throwing things!

PATRICE: Sometimes people do that. You know what people can do. They throw things. That's what people do. They hit. They yell. They behave. It's all *Lord of the Flies*. May I have a cigarette?

GIL: I don't smoke anymore.

(Patrice reaches in Gil's jacket pocket and takes his cigarettes and lighter.)

PATRICE: Stop lying. It's embarrassing.

GIL: It's that Zulu rage, isn't it, Mom? It's that impenetrable African anger that you can't see through. You look at them and haven't got a clue as to what's going on.

PATRICE *(Studying him)*: Do you think that is a particularly *worthy* line to pursue, Gil.

GIL: *Um.*

PATRICE: Let's not make this into some sort of racial test case here.

GIL: I'm not making—

PATRICE *(Cutting him off)*: No, no, no. You are making a critical mistake, sweetie, you are falling right into the traps. That Boer policeman. What he just said before he left: "That's the real African, they're not like your Sidney Poitier kind of native . . ."

GIL: I just said there *is this thing called* Zulu rage, that doesn't make me an Afrikaner!

PATRICE: Well? What's the difference between your two points of view then? It seems to me—

GIL *(Highly agitated and confused)*: But I saw how *violent* she was.

PATRICE: Yes. *True.* But listen. Look. I'm not going to do "the Kafır went mad." I will not lower, *we* will not lower ourselves. What this was, was merely a problem of two personalities clashing, Gil.

GIL: Okay. Big clashing personalities.

PATRICE: I mean, *really* clashing. Because, let's face it, she and I were not over the moon about each other. From the beginning. You had two people coming up against one another. Was it cultural? I'll give you that. Because I wouldn't play mistress to her put-upon servant, and I wouldn't play at being some goddamn lumpy-ankled white Anglican housewife managing her every move, she resented me and she hated *not* being treated like shit.

GIL: But I don't know that she was geared up for a full-fledged insurrection, Mother.

PATRICE: Could we have a drink? And some music? A little something. Because I am still a little . . . *(She laughs)* In shock.

GIL: Why have we been through so many?

PATRICE: What?

GIL: So many servants?

PATRICE: Well, I guess it has been a sort of *festival of maids.* I have to say, it's because I throw them. I'm not what they're used to.

GIL: Do you remember any of their names? I mean, I can barely keep track. It blurs.

PATRICE: Does this in any way, this whole thing, have to do with your brother? It's all so synchronistic with his visit.

GIL: What do you mean?

PATRICE: Well. It's just, sorry to use this expression, but is he "putting ideas in your head?"

GIL *(Offended)*: Please!

PATRICE: Really. Here he comes, the last bastion of the heroes of the left, you know, filled with his inflammatory ideas picked up at Columbia Journalism School, and one can just hear him delivering speeches to Edna—or maybe to *you*—about "When are these people going to take control of their lives?"

GIL: Are you saying he shouldn't talk to people?

PATRICE: Oh please don't paint me as some sort of one-woman police state.

GIL: I'm sorry.

PATRICE *(Very edgy)*: May I have my drink please? I'm done in.

(Gil goes back into the house. Patrice puts out her cigarette in the remains of the Zulu pot.)

Maybe if your brother had been here, I mean, they *like* him. What kind of vacation is it, to not spend even an hour, to not take a shower. He's been here for two days and we've had one meal together and he just split . . .

(Some cool Jobim samba wafts out to the veranda. Gil comes back out with a glass of whiskey for Patrice and water for himself.)

GIL *(Acutely aware of Patrice's fragile state)*: Are you all right?

PATRICE *(Softening)*: I'm so sorry, Gil. To have you part of this. To have you growing up here. We had the idea:

"Oh, let's see the world . . ." This was not at all what one had in mind.

GIL *(Soothing)*: Dad will be home tomorrow. Dad . . . *(He doesn't know what Dad will do. He stops)*

PATRICE: It *really* worries me to hear you put some sort of racial slant on these things.

GIL: I'm sorry, I'm . . . just talking. It's just talk.

    (Beat) Do you ever listen to *Lux Radio Theatre*?

PATRICE: God. I'm not *that* old, Gil.

GIL: Well, it's on here, I lie in bed listening at night. It's probably *new for them,* and—it's, all these awful old English actors pouring drinks all over the place whenever anything slightly sticky happens . . . they're just pouring the whiskey and being civil. Sound effects of ice and stuff in glasses. And screams.

PATRICE *(Looking at the shattered pottery)*: I will grant you one irony. It was not like she was destroying some cheapo Tijuana terra-cotta crap. This was a pot that though very, *very* unattractive, was nevertheless arguably one of a kind. Which counts for *something.* And it's her culture she was smashing, tossing around. And *they* will have been the ones doing the smashing.

GIL: Maybe that's what I was trying to say, that there's an irony.

PATRICE: And come the revolution, you know, and they look around and there's nothing left, I hope they aren't surprised when the only Zulu pot left in the world is in some awful museum. In hell.

(Pause. Gil looks around.)

GIL: I think all the neighbors heard.

PATRICE: Oh yeah, they're all peering out, behind those fuck-ing lace curtains going, "See what that bloody Ameri-can family has gone and done now? They're practically like Jews, they're so loud."

GIL *(Laughing)*: Mother.

PATRICE *(Improvising now that she's getting laughs, she mimes a phone call, this time with a South African/Anglicized voice)*: "Hullo, Mrs. Burgess? This is Mrs. Snitterton from down the road. Just want to say jolly good job, ringing the police. Would you mind sending them by to give my cook a couple of whacks. She made a balls of the beef Wellington and she's being cheeky . . ."

GIL *(Laughing)*: All right, I know.

(Beat. He notices blood on the arm of her dress) There's blood on your sleeve.

PATRICE: It's Edna's. From when the policeman hit her.

GIL *(Anguished)*: Maybe we didn't have to call the police. Maybe that was a bit much.

PATRICE: What else could you do? You did the right thing.

(Pause.)

GIL: Did you see? Did you see how he got the black cop—the black one, mind you—to punch her.

PATRICE *(Tilting her head, listening to the music)*: Listen. You know the great thing about this music? It is infallible. It can not help but to cheer you up. It never fails.

(Hilton enters with a tray, unnoticed, as Patrice begins to dance. She pulls Gil up to join her. Lights fade on the tableau of Patrice and Gil dancing, watched by a silent Hilton.)

Scene 3

The Togo International Airport
Lomé, Republique de Togo, West Africa
The same day

It is late on a torpid, terribly hot afternoon. Harry Burgess enters and passes a Togolese policeman. He looks over his dancers' passports and tickets; Hodges calls to him from offstage.

HODGES: Harry!
HARRY: Ellsworth!

(Hodges enters with suitcase and carry-on bag. Like Harry, he is a rumpled-looking American—clearly a diplomat.)

HODGES: Oh, Harry, I'm so late! Jesus, these flights. Africa. God. The planes? Chicken wire! Crepe paper! Sobbing passengers! Sobbing *pilots*! Finally, we *catch up.*
    (Pointing to the runway, cringing) Look at my plane. They didn't know if the landing gear worked. I mean, there was a quart of fuel left.
HARRY *(Pointing elsewhere on the tarmac)*: Look there. I have to get on that thing in a few minutes. There are bullet marks, you can see them; I think from Entebbe.

(Smiles) Welcome to Togo. This is pretty much it, what you see. There's a nice stamp and railway museum they'll try and show you. But resist. Do.

HODGES: My friend. It's so great to see you. Is there a bar in there? I'd love a Manhattan.

HARRY *(Waving the passports)*: I can't. I've got a plane full of cranky dancers. These planes just take off without warning.

HODGES *(A laugh, smiles)*: I can't believe I missed 'em. I couldn't catch up. But you leave glowing notices in your wake. I hate these trips. There's not enough Valium in the world. My spine! My stomach!

HARRY: Ellsworth. You used to love all the travel. What happened?

HODGES *(Shrugs)*: They've spoilt me. The *New* Washington. Oh God. Carter. I met him. He actually *cares.* The president is standing there looking at you, and you're not, for the first time in a dozen administrations, thinking, What a ghoul, what a *hobgoblin.* I mean—it feels like the Enlightenment!

HARRY: I can't imagine. And I'm in Africa, missing it all.

HODGES: How's Patrice? Is it any easier for her?

(Pause.)

HARRY: She's better. She's doing well.

HODGES *(Unconvinced)*: Yeah.

HARRY: She finally likes Durban. The weirdness eventually turned fun for her. Comedy. It's good. She started work on her book again . . . And Joyce, what about her? Is she—is it true, she's opened a *store* in Georgetown? I never pictured her as a *shopkeeper.*

HODGES: For cooks. Egg cozies and Parisian cocktail shakers at seventy bucks a pop. And Gil? He was this high when I saw him. *(Hodges holds a hand at waist level)*

HARRY: A very interesting boy. Half Lawrence of Arabia, half butterfly collector . . . So—Washington is all yours now, is it? I hear you've redone the office in Revolutionary Blue? Is that true?

HODGES: Well—It *is* like some sort of revolution; the old guard are scared to death. Men with crewcuts sweating. Because Carter has faith. He actually believes in a kind of mystical Jeffersonian nation. He has God, he has them terrified! When they hear the word "culture" . . . they used to just smirk. Now they jump.

HARRY *(Smiling)*: Congratulations on the promotion. Associate Director of Programs and Management. It's daunting.

HODGES: It doesn't come with a pay raise, believe me. Tell me about the dancers.

HARRY *(A favorite subject, and still an amazement to Harry)*: It's a company all descended from a single slave family in Tennessee. They have power. So it hits these people hard. And this tour . . . These kids talking all night. Mixing with audiences after. In Jo'burg, the homelands, Swaziland, everywhere, all over. We were in Sierra Leone . . . and the governments, they don't like it. Because it's all about not taking any crap. But—the people love it. I'm taking them to Durban. Look. Come with us. You'll have the great pleasure of seeing the South African police *vomiting with rage* on the sidelines. It will be . . . heaven. Heaven.

HODGES: The way you have cut through to the Africans. Astonishing. I'm so proud. All the years we were out in the cold: "*The art boys*," they called us, like we were queers—well now I'm the boss. Which is a lot of fun, to my surprise.

HARRY: It may be the Enlightenment. But Ellsworth. I am still out here in—the cold. So to speak.

(*Pressing on*) Two requests for transfer, and two polite responses asking me to please stay on in South Africa. Two! And then silence.

HODGES (*Simple, a shrug*): With the renaming of the agency, we've been preoccupied. We're still sorting it out. The systems are being reshuffled—

HARRY: Ellsworth, please. Not with me. Not that line. Why am I stuck? Should I start thinking about other things?

HODGES: Other things? What else could you do?

HARRY (*Smiling*): It's true. I certainly have no skill at making money, or anything else they do in the real world . . . Ellsworth—what's going on? I've toned down some of the wilder stuff, but—

HODGES: You're a brilliant Africa hand. You have the trust, you have the ears of the Zulus, Xhosas, Muslims. *Muslims,* for God's sake, man! They're still talking about your production of that Thornton Wilder—What was it?

HARRY: *The Long Christmas Dinner*. That was okay. Now I'm going to bring in *Idiot's Delight*. A company from San Francisco, ex- convicts, all of them. And now they're *actors*.

(*There is a muffled Air Afrique announcement.*)

HODGES: Perfect training, wouldn't you say?

(*Beat. He studies his friend*) So what are we going to do with you then? Can you miss your flight; just spend the day with me here? Sort it out? . . .

HARRY *(Shaking his head)*: I can't. I have to get back to Durban. Allie's visiting us. We haven't seen him in two years, and I wasn't there to greet him. If I missed this flight out, it would take me another two days to get home. All the connections.

(Beat, pleading) Why haven't you gotten me out, El? Tell me. Please.

HODGES: Out to where? There were postings in Addis Ababa. Or in Islamabad. You would have *hated* me.

HARRY *(Interrupting)*: There was Buenos Aires. You gave Angus Peterson *Milan*!

HODGES: All right. All right. God, it's so hard to have this conversation on the fly.

(Beat) There's something coming up at Voice of America. You have the background for it: It's a European posting. It's very possible.

HARRY *(After a pause. He is smiling)*: Voice of America? Are you offering it to me, Ellsworth? Is this why you waited? Are you about to make me whole again?

HODGES: At the moment we imagine a magazine show with a free hand. Broad. They want it to be cosmopolitan, Camelot, Cavett-like. Hip. You are an ideal person. An artistic-director-producer type. An impresario. They can't argue with your credentials.

HARRY: Ellsworth. Can you actually get me this thing?

HODGES: It's something you'd be seriously interested in? Before I go to the chief?

HARRY: Yes. We know that. Do you want me to come to Washington and meet?

HODGES: It's a little tricky. We're still accountable to the Old Guard.

HARRY: As always. If you need me to come in with some dog and pony show about fighting soviet propaganda? I'll do it, *fine, if* it gets me the job. I don't mind spouting some party line, I do it all the time.

HODGES *(Reluctant)*: Harry. It's—

HARRY: What—they think I'm a little reddish?

HODGES: It's not quite that simple—Allie. Your boy.

HARRY *(Totally surprised)*: My Allie? What? You . . . ? What about Allie?

HODGES: He's made friends with a group of exiled black South African kids in New York. Most of them are African National Congress. They're very vital, very powerful, and quite secretive. They're a fringe. But educated and worth noting. These are the sorts of people your son will be visiting in Durban.

HARRY: I can't tell him what do to. He's twenty-five years old. He does what he wants.

HODGES *(A gesture of "hold on")*: Wait! We need *access* to them. You're the only person who could open up a dialogue. There is the possibility of some real leadership within that group: Andrew Young whispered in someone's ear that it's going to be some unknown left-field kid who might be Prime Minister one day.

HARRY: So you're saying I should use Allie to draw in his friends? No? Are you? Ellsworth? I'm misreading the situation, right?

HODGES: He is at the nexus. He has an extraordinary vantage point.

HARRY: Nexus. Nexus? Oh. *That word*. This smells. I can smell it. What? Did they come to you? I can't believe it.

HODGES: Harry.

HARRY: Is that the *Old Guard*?

HODGES: It's a very low level of noncovert activity.

HARRY *(Astonished)*: You're asking me to take down names? Make a list?

HODGES *(Exasperated)*: It's not like we're going to give the names to the South African government. It's for us! I'm just asking you to entertain your son's friends. Open a path. A road in. That's the real job.

    (Tired, pleading) Just give 'em something. They'll approve you for VOA. CIA has to sign off, Harry.

HARRY: You think you're one of those guys. Ellsworth, you're not in their league.

HODGES: Nevertheless. I am the Associate Director of Programs and Management. Somehow, they saw fit to give me the corner office.

(Beat.)

HARRY: You have the temerity, the bloody gall to come to me? Did you for a second think I would be your local fuck?

    (Beat, bitter. Ellsworth sighs) Look at you. What have you done to yourself? You're having twelve-ounce steaks and martinis with guys you hate and all just to keep your "Enlightenment" afloat. You knew it was pointless to ask me. Didn't you?

HODGES *(Angry)*: It's this attitude that keeps you out of sight, *thinning out* here in Africa. *(Bitter)* Where you're doing so much *good* for the cause. "Oh he's taking *Burl Ives* on a singing tour o' Somalia." *God.* We laugh when we see your itinerary.

(Beat) We all know that Africa is hopeless. I can get you out.

(Exasperated) This is just like swimming team. Yeah, I once watched you lose a race because you looked back over your shoulder. And you perceptibly *slowed down*. Because you felt bad for the losers. I watched.

HARRY *(Smiles, remembering)*: From the bench. May I remind you. Always second guessing from the bench.

(Testing) Are you still prepared to recommend me for the Voice of America post? Because I'm so *qualified*!

HODGES *(Beat, he looks sad, but affable)*: I should be selling potato shredders with my wife in Georgetown. I keep hoping some big company will come along and offer to buy her out, and we'll have hit it.

(Wistful) The American dream.

(A noise of a plane cranking-up is heard.)

HARRY: That's my flight—

(Beat, knowing) I'm stuck in Durban? . . . If you would just tell me that?

HODGES: Harry, you know how these things work.

(Angry) We're all grownups here.

HARRY *(Leaving)*: Well . . . Ellsworth, have fun at the Enlightenment. Though it sounds to be more in the nature of a good old-fashioned rat-fuck.

HODGES *(Helpless)*: I told them you wouldn't, but I had to ask. *(Beat)* Forgive me.

(Harry walks away toward his flight, leaving Hodges standing by the cyclone fence; another flight is announced.)

Scene 4

Durban, Next morning

The veranda. Allie and Gil enter from the house; Allie carrying the tattered bag full of Edna's possessions seen the night before. The brothers have been arguing. Gil paces anxiously. There is a French café table set up for breakfast, a casual arrangement in the Burgess home.

GIL: Allie, please don't make this into something it's not.

ALLIE *(Exasperated)*: Then what *is* it?

GIL: You don't understand this country. Nothing is what it seems. You can't run around pretending to understand this place when you're just a visitor.

ALLIE: Maybe you would prefer it if there were no questions? If I just accepted . . . There's a woman sitting in the Durban jail.

GIL: Well, you're going to take her her stuff. Ask her yourself. I'm sure she'll tell you what you want to hear.

ALLIE: I am just asking you to create a chronology. It's first-year journalism, try and create a chronology of events—

GIL *(Mock awe)*: Oh boy! A journalism *class*! I'm ever so grateful, do you think I could actually learn, Allie?

ALLIE *(Laughing)*: Okay. I'm a pedant. Fine. I'm still interested in what happens when.

GIL: All right. Edna. Edna. She had worked here for five months. Very nice. No. Not very nice. Just a worker. Not—I would not say . . . happy or sad. Allie. I would say "working."

ALLIE: A blank.

GIL *(Too quick to be trapped)*: No, not a blank. She was just another worker.

ALLIE: And you're saying she just suddenly blew up? Without any signs, without any provocation.

GIL *(Dry)*: It's been known to happen. Here. In this country in case you hadn't noticed. There's a bit of anger. They get quite cross sometimes, or do you think it's all just smoke pot and play guitar on the beach?

ALLIE: Yeah. That's exactly why I came down here. For the . . . partying—

GIL *(Cutting him off)*: Did you say anything to Edna?

ALLIE: Many things.

GIL: Well, what? For instance?

ALLIE: I tried to get to know her. I'm here for two weeks, please don't look at me like that. I wanted to make contact. Have a fucking conversation. Get to know her, her life . . .

GIL: Are you aware of what you do? You treat them like they're all girls that you want to date.

ALLIE *(Scoffs)*: That is so completely disgusting, you're not even my brother.

GIL: I've always seen you do it: "Hullo. I'm cool. You're African. Let's be cool *together* . . ."

  (Beat) But their lives don't get the least bit better

from it. Their lives don't magically improve because you've befriended them on your little holiday. Charmed them. You're like Dad. You are. Exactly.

ALLIE *(Exasperated)*: I don't understand. I talked to her. I didn't suggest she fly to Pretoria and bomb the Ministry of Bantu Affairs or try and beat the crap out of Mom. Look. Edna, she had, *has*, an enormously complicated life. Big problems. Huge.

GIL: Such as?

ALLIE: What do you mean, "Such as?"

GIL: No, I'm just curious.

ALLIE: But, you're not really. All that curious. I mean, if you had been, you'd have asked her.

GIL: And if I had, could I have been of any use? "Oh, a friendly ear?" Please. Allie. It does no good pretending these are your friends. Because they have to do certain things. For instance—get paid. —They have these *jobs*. *I* have been here since I was thirteen. I know something about it.

ALLIE: I would say you know a great deal about it. But what you don't have. What you lack, Gil. Is—you don't have distance.

(Beat) Something has happened to you. Something—

GIL *(Cuts him off. Quiet)*: Please don't tell me. Please don't come here and tell everybody where they don't measure up. Okay? Mother is terrified of you. You know that? Patrice is locked in her room. She's afraid you'll investigate her to death, and judge her and she's not up for it! Nobody wants your brilliant insight, Allie.

ALLIE *(Backing off)*: Okay. You're right. It's unfair. I'm sorry.

(Pause.)

GIL *(Also regretful; conciliatory)*: It must be odd to visit like this.
  We must seem like foreigners to you.
ALLIE *(Looks at his brother; he's pained)*: Gil. You just seem like
  my *brother* to me. My family.
GIL *(After a moment)*: Did you have a nice trip up the coast?
  It's beautiful up there. The beach is amazing. I used to
  explore the tidal pools . . . Did you find your friends?
ALLIE *(Beat. He thinks)*: I have this fairly fucked-up life back
  in New York. Dirt poor. They turned off the lights
  before I left. I'm cold. But what I have is . . . it's mine.
    (Beat) I mean, maybe we could figure this out. You
  could come back with me. To New York. See how that
  works.
GIL: Come back to New York with you.
ALLIE: You could graduate high school in New York, you
  know, with the education you've had here, believe me,
  you're like practically a doctoral candidate by Manhattan standards. Fly back with me.

*(Hilton enters from the house carrying a tray with coffeepot
and cups.)*

HILTON: Good morning! Isn't it a fine morning.
ALLIE: Let me help you.
HILTON: No, thank you, Master Allie. I have taken over the
  kitchen. The garden can wait today. The pool is fine.
  I am of the kitchen.
    (He places the tray on the table) I'm sorry I don't have
  a proper kitchen uniform. Coffee?

ALLIE: Thank you. No, really. Thank you. I can pour my own.

GIL *(To Hilton)*: Please, sure. A bit.

HILTON: Master Gil. I don't know what you like for breakfast. Would you gentlemen care for some eggs and some toast as well? Bacon? Grapefruit? There's a papaya?

ALLIE *(Increasingly tense)*: No, no, no, please. It's fine.

HILTON: I like the kitchen. But don't worry, someone new, someone very good is coming. You're sure you—I saw Edna make French toasts, I'm sure I could if you—

ALLIE *(Under his breath)*: Jesus, Christ. French . . . *(To Hilton)* I—don't really eat until the sun goes down, Hilton, thanks a lot.

GIL *(Sharply, annoyed at Allie—a lesson)*: Hilton, a papaya and a lime, please!

HILTON: Yes.

(Hilton exits into the house.)

ALLIE: So what do you think?

GIL: It's very nice, but I couldn't possibly go back with you. It's impractical.

ALLIE: Oh.

GIL: It's not . . . It's not so simple.

ALLIE: Do you like it here? Do you like your life here?

GIL *(Impatient)*: No. Not in the way you *expect*. Do I like— do you think I'm an idiot? You don't know me, except as someone—you see me once in two years for the first time. —I'm not a child—yes. I like it.

(Beat) What do you think? I could leave Mom here? Alone? In this house? Dad is away three quarters of the year. Do you think that'd be fair, Allie? "Oh, I'm going

home now, with Allie, because it's wretched here . . ."
No. No. Thank you.

ALLIE: Why was Mom arguing with Edna?

GIL: I have no idea.

ALLIE: Her niece's daughter was graduating from secondary school in the Transkei. The first person in their family to attend and complete their schooling. There was a graduation ceremony, not much, probably, from the sounds of it. She showed me a picture of the school which is run by some Jesuits. Mud and dead grass and a few sticks for goal posts, all girls, field hockey and a cross on the roof, but the first in the family, and Edna wanted to go to the graduation but somehow had forgotten to give Patrice enough notice so that when she asked to leave the next morning, for a seven-hour bus trip, Patrice declined.

(Pause.)

GIL: I'm quite sure, I'm pretty sure it is more complicated than that.

ALLIE: I agree. How's school? How's the Blenheim School for Boys?

GIL: Debating. Fencing. Because all the others are off at cricket which I still fail to comprehend after four years.
(Beat) They've made me a prefect, which means I can mete out punishment to younger boys for smoking, or send them to the shop to buy my smokes. It's quite whimsical. The younger boys all rather like me. An exotic. An American. They think of me as "Their American."

ALLIE: I can see how it might be hard to walk away from such riches.

GIL: I'm older now, Allie. I don't need looking after. You needn't take care of me any more.

ALLIE: Looking after? Believe me, New York is a medieval cataclysm, even in the okay parts, and I live in the East Village. You'd just get a futon and a blanket and the rest would be up to you.

(Beat) Listen. Forget it. Forget it even came up, it's just that you seem so . . . this . . .

(Harry enters from the house. He is still in his traveling clothes, haggard and exhausted. There is a moment of both parties taking one another in.)

HARRY *(Shaking his head, taking in Allie)*: *Look* at you guys.

ALLIE: Dad.

HARRY: Oh my God, I keep forgetting you're a grown-up *person.*

(To Gil) Are you happy now? You got your brother.

GIL *(Clearly not)*: Yeah.

HARRY *(To Gil)*: So we had a little problem, huh, with Edna? Did you see that coming?

(To Allie) You weren't here. Huh?

(Patrice enters from the house. She is dressed in a caftan and a large pair of sunglasses are shielding her eyes.)

PATRICE: Was that—was that Hilton? —Did I hear him trying to do breakfast? Is that the noise coming from the kitchen?

GIL: He's done coffee, I think he'll manage, Mom.

PATRICE: Good. At least there's not having to face the kitchen right now. Today. There won't be much in the way of order, it's fend for yourself, meal-wise, not that we were expecting you to join us, Allie. I can't face the . . . mere notion of pots and pans—

HARRY: No, no. We can manage. *(He holds her hand. Smiles)* You don't have to do anything.

PATRICE *(Sitting, distracted)*: They had this table in Antibes. I liked it so much. You can see what the climate—the sea salt—it's starting to rust and you won't be able to get another. I hate to think of what it'll be when we lose this table and these little chairs. I mean, who do you call for a replacement? You can't. Start dialing shops in the Côte d'Azur?

(Hilton comes out of the house. He is carrying the tray. A plate of papaya and limes, two tomatoes and another pot of coffee.)

HILTON: Good morning, madam, Mister Harry!

HARRY: Hilton. Look at you.

PATRICE: Good morning, Hilton. Thank you for jumping in.

HILTON: Look at these tomatoes, just picked, right off the vine two minutes ago. May I make eggs? An omelette?

HARRY: No thanks. The coffee is just fine, Hilton.

PATRICE: Yes, that'll be fine . . . Some juice if there's any left? . . .

HILTON: Yes. Madam. My cousin. Ginger. She can come here at four o'clock for her interview. I called her. She has just left the managing director of Mercedes and she's very talented.

PATRICE: Good.

HILTON: The managing director of Mercedes' wife taught her to make German specialties of the house such as schnitzel and Sacher torte.

PATRICE *(Strained)*: Great. Eva Braun's housekeeper at four, okay.

HILTON: She is not like Edna. Nothing, don't worry . . .

HARRY: What do you mean, Hilton?

HILTON: She favors her employer.

HARRY *(Curious)*: Edna . . . was . . . she had voiced to you some complaint of her treatment or her . . . ?

HILTON: She didn't talk to me. Different tribe. She is different. She is Xhosa. I am Zulu. Different. I can not say what she was thinking.

HARRY *(Pursuing this)*: So, there was no warning here?

PATRICE: Could we, could I just—I would love that juice, Hilton. Maybe we could have breakfast, you know, and not do the post-game discussion for a few hours.

(Hilton goes into the house with the tray.)

HARRY: No, you're right, it's just, I can't get up to speed here, you know, I'm sorry, but I'm—

PATRICE *(Dangerous, a warning)*: Just breakfast!

HARRY: Yes. I only—Fine. Since everyone is okay.
    (To Allie) They—you keep seeing this sort of thing happen—since Soweto the level of violence . . . increasing . . .

ALLIE: What sort of thing?

HARRY *(Carefully)*: Clashes.

ALLIE: Black and white. Servants, masters, that's what . . . you mean?

PATRICE *(Drinks her coffee and speaks carefully and clearly)*: No, Allie. You see something else. You see people not being able to function very well. In any capacity, is what you see, employer or the employed, is what you see, you see. And I will add, that you see it anywhere in the world where people work for other people. You simply hope that you're being quite reasonable in your treatment of one another.

ALLIE: Would you say that your treatment of Edna was reasonable?

HARRY *(Trying to mediate)*: Really, really, let's not do this now, let's go somewhere, get in the car and drive up the coast or . . .

PATRICE *(Cuts him off)*: No, I can answer that. The answer, Allie, is of course not. I do not think my treatment of Edna was reasonable.

(Beat) This situation is not reasonable. Nothing about it exists within reason. No. And was Edna's treatment of *me* reasonable? No. There is no—cogent—Columbia School of Journalism, third-page editorial lesson for you to glean here, as much as I would love to supply one. Because that would be easy.

(Beat) But that's not where we live now. Does that register?

ALLIE: One needn't have servants.

HARRY *(A low, tired moan)*: Allie. Really. Please. Son.

PATRICE *(Relishing this; an increasing gleeful anger)*: Now, that would be a partial solution.

(Beat. More and more excited) We have these functions here, these cultural events. Big crowds. In this house. Big ones. With lots of smoke and little funny foods

and cigars. Because of your father's job, you know, so there's many, many nights, or weekends, when we have the cast of *Pippin* or some local educators or a Minister of Foreign Affairs or Andrew Young or someone else. Okay? So someone has to do the empanada pimiento and sour-cream dip for seventy. So that solution, while, probably no doubt the best, is almost denied one.

(Beat) Also we pay them more than anyone else in the neighborhood and the locals resent us and have to pay more and I'd hate like hell to have to give that up.

(Beat) Maybe an outing of some sort isn't a bad idea.

HARRY: I think so. Drive, some distance. See something we haven't. Some odd Indian mosque.

(To Allie) I was going to show you Ghandi's house.

PATRICE: There's a very, very interesting little monastery in the Drakensberg Mountains where they make crosses out of copper coil.

GIL *(In a kind of scared despair)*: I want to . . . go back . . . to New York with Allie when he leaves.

HARRY: Yeah, but, you have to get back for school, you'd hardly have time to see anything. The Met alone takes four days to take in. And you don't have the time, before turning back around.

PATRICE: I don't think that's what he means, Harry.

(Pause.)

HARRY: Oh. I see. Well. That is certainly understandable, given what you've been through. I think we would all like to leave and—

GIL: I could finish school there. Allie offered. *(Uncertain)* A *futon.*

HARRY: Yes, I'm sure, but it's not practical given the realities. Gil. Come on.

PATRICE: Gil. Kiddo. You know. New York? Come on. His place? Allie's life. I mean, you guys, are you ready for that? That little cold-water place walk-up? . . . You're just—let's not forget your age. Barely seventeen years old and—

GIL *(Desperate, he cuts her off)*: Practically eighteen and you know that I can do fine. My taking care of myself is not at issue! Please!

PATRICE *(Trying for some self-control)*: Look. How do we conduct this talk? I've just had an African woman go mad on me!

GIL: Mother—

PATRICE: No. On us. And we got through it. Now. Now I have pretty much exhausted my capacities to engage, pretty much run down my batteries, and I can not do this one now, not the right way.

GIL *(Almost overwhelmed)*: Dad! I have to—

HARRY: Can't we just agree that we will have this discussion at some point when—

GIL: Of course we can! That's what we— *(He stops; then goes on in a rush)* I can't bear it here, I know that's not helpful to say, I know that's *not*—I was so relieved, when the policeman hit Edna, I was so . . . I liked it.

PATRICE: No, you did not like it. You were glad we were safe.

GIL *(Beyond despair)*: I believe I liked it. I know what I felt. "Good." And you were smiling, Mom . . .

(Pause. Gil tries to collect himself.)

PATRICE: I only have one small question. Allie. The idea of your trip here was that we would—we have a breach—as a family we never communicate. We would try and—the year goes by and we don't write or talk, and the breach widens and you go about your day in New York and we go about our day here and the breach keeps widening and then there's . . . But what are you *doing*?! What are you doing?

ALLIE: I don't know what you mean, Mom. I'm sorry. But I'm not doing—

PATRICE *(Furious)*: Are you telling Gil that he is becoming "just like them"? Assimilating? I would appreciate it if you would stop torturing your brother. It's sadistic and stupid!

HARRY: Oh for Christ's sake, please. All of you. Can't you just—

PATRICE *(Rushing on)*: Please let me sneak—let me talk, Harry. This is fine, this talk, this is needed. Really, darling.

HARRY: No. I am so tired. I can't think. Please. Let me take you inside.

PATRICE *(Cuts him off)*: What's inside? Is it a screening of the new Stanley Kramer? Is it *Guess Who's Coming to Dinner?* Darling, I'm okay, I don't need to go inside. You know, Allie, you have the political instincts of a presumptuous teenage girl! You come here lecturing people on their moral inferiority to you? To you?

HARRY: Stop it, Patrice! Would you just stop!

PATRICE *(Going on, gathering in rage and contempt as she goes)*: Who are you to come down here and play at Che Que-vara? Of The East Village? I read the pieces you send us, and you know what, you have yet to write a single thing that hasn't been said by minds far more unoriginal than your own. You have only smugness to fall back on. Only your own smugness—and it's the smugness of a young man who does not really know what life feels like. Only knows how to play on its disappointments to him. There! Now you know! Who are you to tell Gil? You know nothing of South Africa, baby!

ALLIE *(After a moment)*: What I think is—the problem isn't South Africa. It is you. It's you and Gil and nothing else, and I know everything about that. I know the way it feels, I know what you do to people, how you suck the life out of them. How careful everyone has to be around you, and how much you love that and use it. How you use everyone around you to prop yourself up, no matter how much it hurts them, and I just don't want it to happen to him.

(Beat) That Gil not become a handmaiden.

PATRICE: A handmaiden? Are you actually serious?

ALLIE: Oh yes. That's the one thing I do know. And let's be clear. Your words. This routine. You stopped scaring me when I was twelve.

(Beat) You talk about our breach. That was it. For me. Now. I've said that. And probably we're all thinking—correctly—that this trip was a horrible mistake and wishing it were over, and over it will be. I can go back early.

PATRICE *(Getting up suddenly from the table, screaming)*: Jesus Christ, "handmaiden!" God, that's all the crap I need to hear, fine, go, go back! I can't do this, I'm not going to stand here and do this! You think I'm nuts? That I'd take this? This level of contempt?

ALLIE: No. Nor could Edna, could she?

(Pause. Patrice is shaking. She struggles to speak.)

PATRICE: I can't do this. I have to be careful.

(Patrice runs into the house in tears.)

GIL *(Running after her, crying)*: Please, Mom, I'm sorry, I'm so sorry, really, it's—I'm sorry.

(Harry and Allie are left alone onstage. There is some silence.)

ALLIE: Oh God. Did I do that? I know I promised I wouldn't do this. Did I start that? Do I have to go in and apologize? I can't.
   (Beat) You told me she was . . . She's *not* doing okay. Can't you *see*, Dad? Is it because you're here you can't see? She called the police. On the maid. We don't do that.
   (Beat) I'm sorry, I started that—didn't I? Should I go talk to them?

HARRY *(Shaking his head)*: It's a closed club.

ALLIE: I'll change my ticket.

(Pause.)

HARRY: *No.* No. No.
   (Pause) I'm going to have us out of here within a few months.

ALLIE: You're leaving?

HARRY *(Not able to look at Allie)*: They're finally . . . they're finally giving me Western Europe . . . a posting at Voice of America is what they're offering.

ALLIE *(Amazed)*: Dad, that's huge.

HARRY: Your mother. She'd be fine there. And Gil would be able to move on. She wouldn't need Gil.

ALLIE: Yes. Anything to get them out of here.

HARRY: You *see* that?

ALLIE: *Yes!*

HARRY: Then please. Help me. Stay and help.

(Beat.)

ALLIE: Europe. That's fantastic. That's what you wanted.

HARRY: You *hear* me? *Don't* change your ticket. Help me get us through this time.

ALLIE: How would my staying help?

HARRY: For me! Nobody wants you to leave. We'll clear this away. We'll start over. We can make it good.

(Pause.)

ALLIE *(Not sure what to think)*: All right—

HARRY *(Overlapping)*: You have to be careful. This is not a safe time here. Whatever you may think of all this.

ALLIE: Back to radio. Voice of America! You're not going to be some kind of mouthpiece, are you?

HARRY: No, I can do a lot of good there.

ALLIE: Europe.

HARRY: It's not completely set.

ALLIE: Any sort of change is good. Do it!

(Pause.)

HARRY: God. I want a drink all the time and I never have one. I mean, I have one, but not during decision-making hours.

ALLIE: Which hours are those?

HARRY *(A small smile)*: Between eleven A.M. and noon.

ALLIE *(A small smile back)*: You should try not living with such rigid limitations, Harry.

HARRY: Probably.

ALLIE: A Bloody Mary? That awful hotel down at the beach, the one we stayed at when we first came here, the Oyster Box? Remember? I'm sure the bar is open. It's the only selling point they have. A dark bar. What about it?

HARRY: I can't. I've been on four planes.

ALLIE: Yeah, I have to take this stuff down to Edna anyway. *(Picks up her bag)*

HARRY: Well . . . to be continued?

ALLIE: To be. Yes.

HARRY: Allie, make her bail. *(Hands Allie money)*

(Allie exits.

Hilton returns with his tray; begins to clear the breakfast remains from the café table.)

HILTON: Ginger. Ginger is very adept . . . The butchers and Indian fruit men all know her and save the best for her. They wait for her. Her smile.

(Beat) Edna, you know, she was Xhosa, those people are very bad. Everybody knows . . . They come with bad trouble, always it happens.

(Beat) Ginger is very skilled. She also worked for the—what do you call the person who is the main

teacher at the University of Natal? . . . The . . . ? They wear a black robe?

HARRY *(Absently)*: Uh–huh. Yeah. Here. *(He places a cup on the tray for Hilton)* A chancellor. A dean. A provost.

(Hilton exits. Harry sits alone.)

A boss.

" **ACT TWO** "

Scene 1

The Hague,
Holland, New Year's Eve, 1980

A geometric flat in the manner of De Stijl, circa the early
1920s. The building overlooks a frozen pond. It is cavernous
and austere. In spite of being built to let in light, it is dark.
The furniture is orthodox Modernists—Gerrit Rietveld and
others of the same school.

An elderly Dutch gentleman, Gerrit Van Eden, sits in
black tie, sipping champagne. Patrice is in a dinner dress set
off by a single strand of pearls.

VAN EDEN: I see. So only the one boy lives with you. And
the other?
PATRICE: Lives nowhere, you see. He travels as a sort of life
choice. He's something of a journalist.
VAN EDEN: Ah. Yes. I see. A cultural family then.
PATRICE: Allie, actually, has not done all that much of note.
To tell you the truth. He's sort of a bust. So far. He writes

for the sort of publication where the ink comes off on your dress and you can't get it out: I looked down once and there was an entire interview with Madame Chiang Kai-shek on my frock.

VAN EDEN: Of course, he's still young enough that he has a shot.

PATRICE *(With a kind of manic excitement)*: Well you know, I think I must disagree. We tell young people that they have several chances in life, but actually, Mr. Van Eden, there clearly are very few. Very few. I—when I met my husband, we were both working for a museum. You've probably been to it: The Phillips Collection, American art. In Washington near all the embassies—and I was pursuing a curatorial career. Of course, what, you may ask, does a woman with an interest in American art do when they've just stopped making the stuff?

(Beat) But that's not what we're talking about, is it?

VAN EDEN: Uhm, I can't say I exactly recall. How we got onto.

(Beat) And the boy who lives with you? . . .

PATRICE: Gil.

VAN EDEN: Yes.

PATRICE: What about him?

VAN EDEN: Has he settled on a . . . future?

(Beat.)

PATRICE: I think what you must be referring to is the scandal of his being caught *in flagrante delicto* with that seventeen-year-old boy from the other side of the building?

VAN EDEN *(After a moment)*: No.

PATRICE: Very attractive boy who looks rather like that actor you have—that actor with the eyes. Rutger Hauer. In the room where they store the bicycles. One can understand why one might—an attractive boy.

VAN EDEN: I'm not so familiar with that actor.

PATRICE: Then, of course, you were not part of that petition that was sent round to ask us to move out, to vacate?

(Long pause.)

VAN EDEN: No.

PATRICE: Thank God. I didn't think you, a retired diplomat . . . If you had seen the language they used. The committee. Tenants committee.

> *(Beat)* I thought I saw your name, but perhaps it was a mistake.

VAN EDEN: I believe that my wife, before her illness, was on that body. She had not served for some time.

PATRICE: I can only assume it was a problem with translation. Words like "preying on," and "predatory perversion." These words must have other, alternative meanings in Dutch. I was surprised to see how bigoted and small-minded our neighbors were. I thought this was a progressive culture where such things—

VAN EDEN *(Cautious but interrupts)*: I do not follow the various . . . comings and goings. Of the area. People are free to live their lives as they wish.

PATRICE *(Touched, surprised)*: Thank you. Yes. I agree.

> *(Beat)* As for Gil. I don't care what he does. None of that bothers me. If he were here he could speak to this

issue himself. For instance. The idea of service. —That is something young people no longer appreciate.

VAN EDEN: Service?

PATRICE: Well—how can you develop a notion of service when you don't give a fuck? When you're entirely indifferent to propriety and the needs of others.

VAN EDEN: Oh yes.

PATRICE: Why should they want to serve anything at all when they have no reason to respect any of the institutions offered to them?

VAN EDEN *(Proceeding gingerly)*: I do disagree, with all respect, having spent my life as a diplomat, just like your husband. When I was the governor of Suriname, the younger generation, even if they were opposed—

PATRICE *(Cuts him off)*: But you lost it. The Dutch lost Suriname, right?

(Pause.)

VAN EDEN: Yes. It had been coming for years. I ran it as best—

PATRICE: Yes, I'm sure you ran it wonderfully. I'm quite certain all the trains ran on time. But did the Dutch—but did you provide the Surinamanians with a good example before they threw you out?

VAN EDEN *(Correcting her gently)*: Surinamese.

PATRICE: The point I'm getting at is that on the one hand there is the notion of service, and on the other protest, fighting—somewhere in between the two is stasis. In other words: Gil. Of course what example are *we* giving him? You know, you live downstairs, so you hear these horrible parties we have to give. For visiting artists. I mean, if I had to listen to Philip Glass all day, I'd want to give blowjobs in the bike room too.

VAN EDEN *(After a moment)*: Yes.

PATRICE: Have you ever heard, actually heard, Harry's program on Voice of America?

VAN EDEN: I've missed it, I'm afraid.

PATRICE: Culture. *American Culture Now.* Is the show. Different events each week. If it's theatre, it's always some blue-collar thing with a porch and a broken dog. If it's art, it's always a sort of primitive thing with a despairing Laotian. And then they all come over here for a sweet-and-sour pupu platter.

VAN EDEN *(After a moment)*: Indeed.

PATRICE: Of course, we'll all look back on this as the *golden age*, compared with what's to come. What with this stiff new broom in Washington it will all be different. It's all up for grabs now. Of course one prays he's a better president than he was a movie star but politics are easier, don't you agree?

(Gil enters. He's somewhat unsteady on his feet. He's grinning. Van Eden stands.)

GIL: Hello!

(Beat) Oh. They're not here yet? Wow. I'd have thought. By now. Hi.

PATRICE *(Taking note of his condition)*: Yes, just think, you could have stayed wherever you were for another hour or so and had so much more fun. Think of all the fantastic fun you missed!

GIL: Oh well. There's . . . always tomorrow, right?

PATRICE: The airport, the snow, your father called, they're delayed, he's waiting. Gil, you haven't met Meneer Van Eden from downstairs, have you?

GIL: In the lift once, I believe. Hi.

VAN EDEN: Hi. Happy New Year.

GIL: Let me just tell you, it's very festive out there. The bars. Wow. I actually saw two guys in one of them. Laughing! Can you imagine? Roaring! Of course the bartender shot a disapproving glance, and they went back to their Vermeer silence. But for a moment there . . . *(Gil does a mocking little disco step or two)* It was Studio 54.

PATRICE: I'm sure it was a ball. We were discussing the problem notion of service. Service to others. Anything outside oneself.

GIL *(A moan)*: Again? Oh. I'm so sorry, Mr. Van Eden.

PATRICE: I've become repetitious, Mr. Van Eden, according to Gil.

GIL: Did you get to the part yet where you talk about the "pseudo-suburban-artistic frauds"? Or did I miss that? 'Cause that's usually good.

PATRICE: Gil is no doubt referring to my position on the types of artists championed by Voice of America.

GIL: And when some—and I quote—"plaintive rural shriek" floats down to your flat—

PATRICE: You can be certain we're having a recital, and that I can be found quietly sobbing in the loo.

GIL: Yes, usually, that's pretty much where you can be found.

(Beat.)

VAN EDEN: May I have some more of this lovely champagne?

PATRICE: Like you guys did in Suriname, I lost a certain amount of credibility with Gil after I beat the shit out of our African maid. Didn't I, darling?

GIL: Yes. But she's very credible now.

PATRICE *(Pours for Van Eden)*: Well, Gil, maybe you can help from a young person's perspective.

GIL: I doubt it.

PATRICE: Perhaps you could shed some *light*?

GIL: Not likely.

PATRICE: *Why is it* that the young dancers and the choreographers Harry brings around, and the poets, and the writers—the same trotting out of their same six discoveries. "The story of me and my crisis." Part eight hundred and thirty-seven. The complaining, the lack of courage. The special pleading.

GIL: The young people I know don't complain much at all.

PATRICE *(A short laugh)*: I'll bet they don't. We are aware of that. Everyone in the *building* is aware of that.

VAN EDEN *(Suddenly understanding the parameters of what he may be trapped in)*: Do you think you might have anything stronger than champagne? *(Patrice smiles at him— the perfect hostess)*

PATRICE: It was so nice of you to accept our invitation to spend New Year's Eve with us! Such a special night! I usually like to spend it alone. But since we have Allie and his new girlfriend—there's a dozen blondes a year, and I don't know if we're on Miss January or if it's still Miss December. —Did you ask for something harder?

VAN EDEN: Vodka, madame, if it's no bother.

GIL *(Eager)*: Vodka, good idea. I'll get it. Let me.

PATRICE: Well. Why don't I bring out the caviar? A gift from a defecting Estonian poet my husband helped. He wrote a poem about a cow. It was thirty-six minutes long.

(In a mock Eastern European accent)

Here are my swollen,
glistening,
shit-encrusted
udders!
Your Motherland!
Your swamp!

(Beat.)

VAN EDEN: . . . Very nice.

PATRICE: Well, *I* was moved.

    (Beat) May I ask you something?

VAN EDEN: Of course.

PATRICE: Your wife. Your beautiful wife. I used to talk to her. When we first moved in. And she was *very* stunning. Did you *love* her? Did you love her *very* much?

VAN EDEN: Yes.

PATRICE: When was it that she died? I didn't realize she had been so ill! I always wanted to have that look—she had that look-of removal, radiant removal so useful for diplomatic wives and I never could get it. I'm so sorry we never got a chance to get to know one another. We would surely have been friends. —When did you say?

VAN EDEN *(After the smallest beat)*: Six weeks. It's six weeks ago. She had been ill for quite some time as you know, so——

PATRICE *(Excited)*: Wait! Wait! Let me get the sevruga! ——Please, please tell me all about her. I can't wait.

(She exits. Van Eden and Gil look at each other.)

GIL: I'm sorry, I'm so sorry.

VAN EDEN: Are you enjoying Holland, young man?

GIL *(His eyes closed)*: I'm sorry. Please, it's——sometimes she doesn't know that she's saying things which are not allowed.

VAN EDEN *(Kindly)*: Not at all. I don't mind at all. Now. My question was, are you enjoying The Netherlands?

(Beat.)

GIL: A lot. The museums. The art. The paintings.
    (Beat) The Dutch landscape. I've been working my way through it. It could take a lifetime.

VAN EDEN: Yes. Beautiful. This particular green——nowhere else quite so, in the world.

GIL *(Walking to the window)*: Yeah. But you know, what I like, was . . . the——I've been looking at a lot of Mondrian. Because there are so many here.

VAN EDEN: Mondrian. Yes. I must say, I don't care for him.

GIL: I do. A lot. He started off . . . he started off painting trees. And the green you mention——he knew it, he caught it. And then something happened.
    (Beat) A volte-face. An abrupt turn. And he left everything behind, and stripped the world to its essential.

(Beat) By the end of his life, the thought of green simply revolted him. It didn't fit in. And he was right. Reduce the magnificent Dutch landscapes of the seventeenth century, those architectural views, the pictures of people living life in moving pastoral settings, and then reduce the sentiment, reduce the feeling, and continue. Until you get to Mondrian. *(Beat. Looks out)*

VAN EDEN *(Looks out the window, smiling)*: Hmm. I can't see that. I still see what I see. A frozen pond. Green trees. I should look more closely.

GIL *(Tentative)*: If you wanted to see some Mondrians. They have the largest collection in the world. The Gemeente Museum——?

VAN EDEN: An outing would be lovely. Of course. Any time. I haven't been in that museum in decades.

(There is a moment.)

PATRICE *(Returning with caviar)*: Mr. Van Eden, one gets so seldom to speak to people of a certain wit——please——I want to know if you were expatriates. We have *so* much in common. Is it all right to ask? How did she die?

VAN EDEN *(Takes a deep breath)*: Yes. Fine. Mrs. Burgess. When we were in Suriname, she contracted malaria.

(Beat) And in the old days, in Suriname, in Paramaribo, we used to have fireworks on New Year's Eve. Just like those you shall see tonight at midnight. And I would arrange these fireworks displays because she missed home, you see. But in Suriname, the fireworks would go off, and there would be a flash of light on

jungle. Not on this glorious Dutch landscape we called home. When I retired, she wanted to come back here. Home. Even though the chill of this lowland was very bad for her.

(Beat) There is no land more wet, more damp, for here, as you know, we are below sea level, under the sea, really.

(Beat) Before she died, Mrs. Burgess, my wife said to me, "Gerrit, there is no more harbor. No more port. We are sailors on the *Flying Dutchman*, ancient mariners on a boat, always at sea."

(Sound of elevator is heard offstage.)

PATRICE *(Wildly enthusiastic at the sound of the elevator)*: Listen! He's here! Your brother's here! Get the champagne ready.
GIL *(Calming)*: Mom.
PATRICE *(Looks at herself; then runs to the door)*: Oh God! This outfit.
HARRY *(Enters)*: Sorry we're so late.

(Harry is more gray, more expansive, more prosperous, in a Bond Street cashmere overcoat. He takes in Van Eden, whom he does not appear to know.)

Oh. Hello! Gee. Company.
PATRICE: You're alone!
GIL: Hey. Where's Allie?
HARRY: They're here. They went to the corner. He said he had to go see a canal.
GIL *(Exiting)*: Jesus, a canal?

HARRY *(Calling after him)*: But bring them back, because your mother's waited long enough.

PATRICE *(To Van Eden)*: This is my son Allie's modus vivendi. He exquisitely delays the pleasure of seeing me.

HARRY: No. He wants his girl to see—

PATRICE *(A dismissive grunt, cuts him off)*: Uh-huh. Uh-huh. This is Mr. Gerrit Van Eden, the neighbor I mentioned. The retired governor of Suriname.

HARRY: Ah! Yes, of course! Good to meet you. Finally.

PATRICE: Have you heard anything? Any news from . . . Washington on the hostages? Any high-flying telexes?

HARRY: Nothing yet. Nothing on the wire services. Just the same old "any day now" . . . Rumors abound.

PATRICE: Of course, the second Carter is on that helicopter off the White House lawn, the second he's gone. They'll be free. Because Reagan made a deal. It's so clear to me.

HARRY: Any way that gets 'em out, fine with me. So what?

PATRICE: Meneer Van Eden. My husband and I have not fought as much in years as we have over this last election.

HARRY *(Laughing)*: We didn't fight, Patrice. I was right and you were wrong.

PATRICE *(Hands him a gold envelope)*: And look what came today, Harry.

HARRY *(Peering at the envelope)*: Huh. Well.

PATRICE: Isn't that exciting?

HARRY *(Slightly self-mocking)*: They approve of me. Very good sign. Very good.

PATRICE: Our invitation to the Inauguration! Mr. Van Eden. Isn't that wonderful? One only hopes one gets to sit near Bob and Dolores Hope.

HARRY *(Jovial)*: You know, come on, it's unfair to presume these people are all philistines and country club boors, sweetie. It's just such a—that's so old. That's so *un-hip*. I'm sure they're the usual mix of the usual sorts of people. Some worse than others.

PATRICE: Huh! I'll say.

HARRY: I passed a little farm stand on the way. *(Hands her a small bag)* Those hothouse tomatoes you like. A fortune. But here. Happy New Year, baby. You're going to love this one. Scuttlebutt on the Rialto is that Disney's coming. They want to build a European Disneyland!

PATRICE: Well, It is a small world after all.

HARRY: Well, it's the ideal cultural export. It makes perfect sense—

PATRICE *(Interrupts, upset)*: How long does it take to look at a frozen canal? This is a deliberate message.

HARRY *(Lightly)*: Then we just don't take the bait, honey. I'm warning you, Mr. Van Eden, my son can be something of a pugilist. Especially with diplomats.

PATRICE: Oh, no match for Meneer Van Eden, though. You know, his wife was on that committee. You know? The tenants committee? On un-American activities?

HARRY: Oh. Oh. I see. Well.

PATRICE *(Cheerful)*: But she'd not been active on it in some time. Well. I'm going to cut up these very expensive hothouse tomatoes into translucent, artful little slices.

(Patrice exits.)

VAN EDEN *(After an awkward moment)*: I know nothing of the petition your wife mentioned, Mr. Burgess.

HARRY: Thank you. I—thank you. Not a pleasant experience with those people.

VAN EDEN: Are you enjoying this posting, Mr. Burgess? You've been here—what is it—a year and a half?

HARRY *(Uneasy)*: Oh yes. It's lovely. The Hague is lovely. So quiet. Look. I apologize—my wife. Patrice, it's not easy to—

VAN EDEN: Would you prefer it if I left? I do have several excuses at hand, you know. My dalmatians require attention. My sadness at being with a happy family on New Year's Eve. One could slip away.

HARRY: It's a kind offer, but please stay.

VAN EDEN: In . . . your line of work, where men spend so much of the day simply lying, I find the truth rather a tonic. She is not well, is she?

HARRY: Tonight it's worse. Our older boy arriving. Republicans move into the White House. She feels . . . that in particular agitates her.

VAN EDEN: But not you?

HARRY *(Sitting)*: I have learned, maybe a little late in life, the essential lesson for all diplomats: "Stay out of the way of the politicians."

VAN EDEN *(Laughs)*: Oh, yes.

HARRY: "Beware the wise men when they come limping into sight." One of those Chinese proverbs. I duck 'em.

(*He laughs*) It's so much cleaner that way. My wife likes to create a little fiction that I'm a closet conservative. But I'm purely a *conservator*. Whoever's in charge, they're still gonna need a little culture.

(*Hears elevator noise from off*) That'll be the kids.

(Allie enters, holding the hand of a girl, Carly, who is quite beautiful, quite blonde, and quite strong looking. Gil follows.)

ALLIE *(Taking the place in)*: *Amazing* house. Pure modernist, huh? Not a decorative lowering of the guard anywhere. What a place. You know. You could live here and you could very very quickly dispense with all the prefatory emotions. And get down to brass tacks.

(Patrice enters.)

Hello, Mother.

(There is a moment between them. She hugs him, and in that moment, her guard drops.)

PATRICE: Hello, sweet one. Look at you. Look at you. My God. The Bohemian life? You could become a diet guru: the Bohemian Diet. And you're Carly Fletcher.
CARLY: Hi. Yes.
PATRICE: We have champagne glasses. We have champagne!

(Patrice pours the champagne into glasses and passes them around.)

HARRY: This is Meneer Gerrit Van Eden. He has a most distinguished, legendary diplomatic career behind him. Which I'm sure you'll ask him about, won't you, Allie?
ALLIE: Good to meet you, sir. We're privileged—more tribesmen. This town is crawling with diplomats.
(To Carly) Be careful of what you say. God knows where it may end up.

CARLY: Alec. Cool it. Chill out. Relax.

ALLIE: You think I should? What would happen if I did? If I did that, the entire world would crumble like an applebrown betty.

CARLY: Okay, whatever.

PATRICE: Harry. Will you do the honors?

HARRY: Over to you. My toasts have come to sound like public service announcements.

PATRICE *(Toasts)*: Allie. To your safe arrival. To peace breaking out. To a long, long, fruitful life *(Looking at Gil pointedly)* none of it wasted, none of it misused. To health. To grace . . . *(She falters)*

HARRY *(Stepping in)*: And to the safe return of the hostages.

PATRICE *(A wry laugh)*: Well, that's a forgone conclusion at this point, sweetie, but what the hell.

ALLIE *(Holding up his glass)*: To family. To being . . . a *family*. Cheers.

(They drink.)

CARLY: Wow. French champagne tastes so different in Europe.

HARRY: Yeah. They save the best for themselves.

PATRICE: Why were you so late?

ALLIE: The airports. The sport of blowing up Westerners. It's a hobby. Very inconvenient. You have to add on an extra hour for every bomb that goes off somewhere.

HARRY: There was actually a little confusion over the flights. They came—

ALLIE: You didn't tell her?

PATRICE: What?

ALLIE: We changed flights. We didn't just come from New York. We came from Johannesburg.

HARRY *(Smiling in a shrug to Patrice)*: I forgot to tell you.

PATRICE: From South Africa? You were in—

ALLIE: I had to go back. A story.

GIL: You were just in South Africa?

HARRY: God knows, you've got an amazing perspective on the place.

ALLIE: Not amazing. Just a realistic one, actually, Pop.

GIL: I have to tell you, I swear, I have no intention of ever, ever setting foot back in South Africa as long as I live, so help me God.

CARLY *(To Patrice)*: I reminded him to . . . call you from Durban to tell you that we changed it, but of course he forgot, so poor Mr. Burgess was waiting . . . at the wrong terminal for the wrong plane.

HARRY: You've been in Durban too?
    (Beat) Is it the same?

GIL: Why did you go to Durban?

ALLIE: It was an impulsive decision. I thought, If not now . . . when? I thought I saw the makings of a story. So we left a few days early.

PATRICE: So do you? Have a story?

ALLIE: I don't know yet. I think so. I think I might.

(He looks at Harry. Harry is relaxed.)

HARRY: Well. Tell us then. Tell us who's doing what to whom at the moment.

ALLIE: Why don't you go first, Carly? Tell about the animals and the sights and then I'll go.

CARLY: We saw many things. Amazing things. Takes your breath away. The natural beauty? Astonishing.

VAN EDEN *(Encouraging)*: Go on, young lady. Tell about the many things.

CARLY *(Careful)*: Well, I didn't see what Al saw, so I can't exactly say. But for me it was—I'm more interested in nature than Allie, you know, the natural world and all, the environment, the game parks, so, while he was doing his journalism thing, I like, you know, went on a day trip to the game park and watched the lions.

GIL *(Incredulous)*: The lions? You went sight-seeing?

ALLIE: Don't underestimate the value of the many lessons to be learned from lions. When they fight for dominance, they don't just kill their enemy. They kill their off-spring as well. And while Carly was learning from the lions, I did my "journalism thing." Old friends. Old haunts. Contacts. See who's left. What's right.

(Beat) Mr. Van Eden. My girlfriend told me she thought it was the most beautiful place she'd ever seen. And I thought, How can this relationship ever work? She sees beauty. I see bodies.

CARLY: Allie—

VAN EDEN *(Getting up, has had enough)*: Well then. I think I hear my dalmatians crying out for a nice walk around the pond. It's been lovely. Good night.

(He walks toward the elevator) Mr. Burgess. A pleasure. Mrs. Burgess. If I don't see you around the mailbox, good-bye.

(To Gil) Our expedition. I look forward to it. Any time. The Mondrians.

(He leaves.)

GIL: *How to Clear a Room: A Step-By-Step Manual,* by The Burgess Family.

PATRICE: Honey. I'm sure it's awful. I can't even look at the words "South Africa" in the paper. I can't see them. I avert my gaze. I just can't. You know

ALLIE: Anyway, I can't go back. They kicked me out, so, it's fine.

PATRICE: They expelled you?

HARRY: The South African government expelled you?

ALLIE: Yes, for my own safety. I mean, one would think that expulsion would be an impediment to a journalist who had staked out South Africa, and made it his own ostensibly private mandate, but actually, it didn't much matter. When it comes to South Africa, I'm not much of a journalist. I can never get anyone to talk to me.

PATRICE: I'm sorry, Allie. It takes time. These things.

ALLIE: It has been the most *baffling* thing. The most *inexplicable* thing, Mom. Because I'm good. I've got Harry's eye for detail and Patrice's nose for liars. And I would get asked to write about the uprisings, and all my contacts dried up. No South African I knew in New York would talk to me. Dropped me.

   (Beat) It started a few months after my last visit to you there. That terrible time? When we were all crazy? . . .

HARRY: Oh Allie. Please. It's New Year's Eve.

PATRICE: No. Go on. I want to hear this.

ALLIE: Okay. So. I thought, Well, why not go down there and find out why all my old friends would no longer talk to me.

CARLY *(A laugh)*: Being that it's on the way to Holland and all.

ALLIE: My friends, who happened to be black, as you might recall, Patrice, Harry. And I found out exactly why. You met them all. Kalia Nogobene. Julian Mapotani. Hank Singh, Andrew Mofolo, Julie Tlali. Lionel Sepopa. Eight or so. That had been to our house. And we—if you recall—we had talked. Long into the nights, drinking, remember? Talk of the future?

PATRICE: Alec, what are you saying?

ALLIE: That those people are all either dead or in jail.

CARLY *(Almost inaudible)*: You didn't tell me that.

GIL: They were all taken in? Those exact people?

ALLIE: The one's who came to our house. And I was the only thing that all those people had in common. They weren't on lists—

HARRY: Everybody there is on a list.

ALLIE: Not together! Not the same ones! These people, they didn't *know* each other, they didn't turn in the same circles, they were not all part of some cell. Kalia Nogobene's sixteen-year-old sister that she brought with her?

(Beat. Furious) I was the *only* thing they had in common.

HARRY: Alec. You can't blame yourself.

ALLIE *(Looking at Harry)*: I don't.

GIL: Therefore?

ALLIE: What did I tell you. What was the lesson? Journalism 101.

GIL: A chronology.

HARRY: Which leads to?

ALLIE *(Simple, heartbroken)*: All roads lead to home, Harry. To Dad.

PATRICE: What are you saying, Allie?

HARRY: Wait. Why would that have anything to do with me?

(Beat.)

ALLIE: Pop. Dad. Did you give our government a list?

PATRICE *(Astonished)*: What?

ALLIE: Please. Tell me. Just tell me—was there something . . . said?

HARRY: Son.

ALLIE *(More and more sure)*: There had to have been a list. There had to have been a link between me—and them—and you—

PATRICE *(Interrupts)*: *No.* No. No. This is not a game to be played in our house ever again. We are not doing this again.

HARRY: Why did you bring people to our home if you thought I was some sort of—why would you—

GIL *(Overlapping)*: He didn't, Allie. He wouldn't. Dad. You're not that sort of man.

ALLIE *(Pressing)*: Tell me I'm wrong. Dad. You encouraged me to invite people into our home.

PATRICE: We are not going to rise to the bait!

HARRY: I worked day and night to try and effect some scant trace of decent human behavior down there! I did everything in my power to run counter to the indifference of our *own* government. I was the only one who ever even raised his voice! God, what do you think of me? How could my own son think me capable of such—do you hate me that much? Allie?

ALLIE *(More convinced)*: You warned me! You told me it was
    dangerous. You didn't tell me you were the dangerous
    one.

    (Beat) In Durban. At the hotel. The Oyster Box, I get
    death threats. In New York. People would spit at me.

    (Beat) There had to have been a list

HARRY: But, Son, whatever you thought, if you'd come to
    me and asked—

ALLIE: Have you forgotten how to tell the fucking truth?

HARRY *(Gaining in fervor, desperate to be persuasive)*: Whatever
    it is, whatever happened, you must understand, the
    levels of complexity—I would never do anything that
    put anybody at risk. You can't possibly believe that of
    me. We're talking about a treacherous country in the
    midst of revolution. Any number of polluted sources
    could have—

PATRICE: Stop it, Harry.

HARRY *(Still trying to hold on)*: Something must have—

PATRICE *(Cuts him off. Sharp and vivid)*: Stop it, right now,
    stop. Just stop!

    (Beat) Is that why you got promoted so suddenly,
    Harry? Because I have never figured it out. We were
    not on the fast track, my sweet. You were floundering.
    We were set for the Third World forever.

GIL: I refuse to believe this. I won't.

    (Beat.)

PATRICE: Is that why they gave you Europe? Because you
    finally gave them something? Harry. Come on now.

HARRY: Don't look at me like that! None of you have the right to look at me like that. Have you forgotten what was happening there?

(Beat.)

You benefited from . . . You all . . .

(Pause.)

PATRICE: So you gave them a piece of paper, Harry? Did you type it? . . . Your list?

HARRY *(Almost a whisper)*: There was never a . . . list. There were just conversations.

GIL: Dad.

HARRY *(Rage and exhaustion)*: I had to get us out. *(Yelling)* I had to get us out, goddamn it!

PATRICE: It's the end of the world, isn't it? Harry. Darling.

(Beat.)

We've done it.

(Allie stands there, sobbing. Lights fade.)

Scene 2

A few hours later

Allie sits in the near dark. It is snowing. He stares out at the falling snow. The radio is on, a fuzzy Voice of America broadcast. Strange wailing music warbles out, and ends.

HARRY *(On the radio)*: And that was "Awaken the Day" sung by the Black River Mountain Appalachian shaped-note singers, who will be in Reykjavik on January 2nd, 4th and 18th. This is Harry Burgess. Stay tuned for our New Year's Eve celebration of Negro spiritual music from the Civil War and beyond. But first, news headlines from VOA's news service.

ANNOUNCER *(Over fuzz and static and an excited crowd)*: This is the Voice of America, and it's going to be a clear night in Manhattan, with temperatures in the low twenties, people already coming together for the annual ritual of watching the descent of the ball in Times Square, as the new year arrives. In Washington, President Carter is spending the last hours of 1980 awaiting word on terms for the freeing of the fifty-two American hostages, while President-Elect Reagan, emerging from church this morning in Bel Air, dubbed the Iranian kidnappers "barbarians."

GIL *(Entering; over the above)*: I can't seem to rustle up a cab. It's too close to midnight. The New Year's Eve thing. All the cab drivers must be off.

(Gil turns the radio off. He looks at his frozen brother)

Come on Allie. We've got to start moving. Carly is at the corner, trying to get a cab.

ALLIE *(Looking out the window)*: Gil. Can you skate on that pond?

(Gil studies his motionless brother for a moment.)

GIL: It's too small. You'd just have to stand there.
　　(Beat.) Allie. I've packed, I just don't know if I got everything I need. What do I need?

ALLIE: A coat.

GIL: A coat?

ALLIE: A sweater. A T-shirt. Some jeans. Something to read. that's it. Always bring a book. Does she know?

GIL: Yeah. I told her. Through her door. She wouldn't open it. But she heard. She didn't say anything. I don't think she's going to come out. I don't think she's even going to say good-bye.

ALLIE: You know, Gil. I've been thinking about luck. There's never enough luck in a family, to go around. Maybe you got it all. I hope so.

GIL: What do you mean? You can't think that way.
　　(He goes to Allie to help him get up) Come on. We've got to go.

CARLY *(Entering, snow covers her overcoat)*: I have a cab. I had to lie to him—he doesn't want to take us to the airport or anything like that. But maybe he can be like coaxed or something.

> *(Beat. A small grin)* He takes credit cards so I can give him my dad's. He lets me keep it for like emergencies and stuff. I buy presents and he never notices.

ALLIE: I really wanted to skate on a canal.

GIL: I don't think there's time.

CARLY: Come on, Allie. Just get up and follow us. You don't have to do anything. You don't have to think. You just have to move. If you don't want to go back to New York, we'll go somewhere else.

GIL: What did you have in mind?

CARLY: Anywhere. Spain. A beach. It's warm there. We'll thaw you out.

ALLIE: Thaw me out . . . *(He laughs)*

CARLY *(Helping him to his feet)*: Come on, Pal.

ALLIE *(To Carly)*: I think I lost my passport somewhere along the way, Carly. Today. I don't know where. *(He grins)*

CARLY: I have it. See? We'll be fine.

(Harry enters. Carly, seeing him, tries to lead the frozen Allie out.)

Come on Allie, let's go.

HARRY: Gil. Can you talk to your mother? She's locked herself in. She won't come out.

GIL: I tried. It's no use.

CARLY: Come on Allie—let's go . . . The cab is . . . he won't wait.

HARRY *(Crosses to Allie, pleading)*: I was told we were offering help to people who would need it in the future.

ALLIE: Harry.

HARRY: In the future. I was told that new doors were being opened and that it was—

(Beat.)

ALLIE *(A small sad smile)*: Harry. Don't you know? Look at me. You've killed me. Don't you understand that? Don't you want to say *good-bye*?

HARRY: I am not one of those men!

ALLIE: Clearly. They, Harry, are much better at it than you. If you had been one of "those men," I would have never found out.

    (Pause. Softly laughing) I was so careful never to take anything from you. No money for college, nothing to make me feel guilty. Why? Why did I bother?

HARRY *(Pleading)*: Allie, please. For God's sakes . . .

PATRICE *(Entering)*: Harry. They should go now! Let them. Just let them go. It is better that way.

ALLIE *(He looks at Patrice and Harry)*: Good-bye . . . Mom.

(Pause. She does nothing.)

It needn't have been, you know. There are *so* many other ways to live.

    (He turns to Gil) Let's go.

GIL *(Indicating Harry and Patrice)*: I just have to . . . I need to . . .

ALLIE: Go ahead.

(Allie and Carly wait by the door.)

GIL: Dad?

HARRY: I see how scared you are, but you will find moments where you have to take action. And who knows all the consequences. To examine every action. That would drive you mad. You cannot dwell.

> *(Beat)* Gil. It's random and unknowable. But you still have to keep . . .

GIL *(Interrupts)*: Your coat.

HARRY: What?

GIL: Your coat. I know it's expensive but I need to take it, you see, mine is at the cleaners, I wasn't expecting to need it, and I can't get it back now that we're . . . so I promise I'll send it back to you. I need a coat.

HARRY: No. It's fine. That's all right. You could keep that coat. I have another.

GIL: I'll send it back. I just need something to keep warm. I don't know where we're going—

HARRY: There's a scarf and gloves in the pocket.

GIL: Thanks.

HARRY: I understand why you might be inclined towards loathing me.

GIL: If only I had loathed you. *That*, at least, would have been a feeling. It would have been *something*.

> *(Turns to Patrice)* Mother?

(She doesn't respond.)

I know how important the idea of service is to you, Mom. But I can't do it anymore.

PATRICE *(After a moment)*: Well, I hope, I really hope, that wherever it is that you're going, they have a sympathetic tenants committee. 'Cause we won't be there to bail you out.

(Gil, Allie and Carly exit.
Long pause.)

HARRY: They'll be all right. They'll take care of each other.

(Patrice listens to the sound of the descending elevator for a moment.)

PATRICE *(Listening, stricken)*: Listen. I often sit here, you know, Harry, wondering when you're going to be home, and wait for that noise. And it made me so happy, to know you'd come back again, which I never expected—"Oh boy, he didn't fly the coop." That noise—I never imagined it could suddenly mean something so horrible, Harry . . . *(She is quietly crying)*

HARRY *(Quiet, absent)*: I want . . . the first little house we lived in back then. That we rented for a year when I was teaching—that's where I want to live. A very small space. No mail. One of those mailboxes at the end of the road, perhaps, but I wouldn't walk to it, I wouldn't check it . . .

PATRICE *(Very quiet)*: What's going to happen to you, Harry?

HARRY: We should have stayed home. In the first place. All of us. To have imagined that we could do anything decent with the world . . .

PATRICE *(She goes to him)*: Let me put you to bed, Harry.

HARRY: Why? Do you still love me, Patrice?

(Beat. She says nothing.)

Maybe I'll just stay here for a bit. I'm not tired yet.

(Harry walks over to the radio and turns it on. It's a Voice of America announcer.)

ANNOUNCER: The Carter-Reagan transition team still in a closed door session. There's no further word from Tehran. This has been a Voice of America news brief. *(Music)*

HARRY *(Remote)*: Poor Carter. Nothing he ever did worked. He could never do the right thing. And he just kept trying and trying and trying.

ANNOUNCER: It is six P.M. in New York, six hours until the end of the year. This is the Voice of America.

(Over the pond, over The Hague, there is a sudden flash of fireworks. The sky turns red.
Harry and Patrice look out.)

HARRY: Happy New Year! Patrice!

Scene 3

Southern Mexico, 1987

The dig sight. It is very late, just before the first bit of light begins to turn the darkness over. Gil is sitting near a fire. He has loosely assembled a section of the pot. Sounds of rustling in the darkness.

GIL *(Under his breath)*: Oh Shit! Forget it! *(Shouting into the darkness)* Go. Olvida! Aqui muy peligroso. Hay una pistola. Jesus. Go! There's nothing here. *(Beat)*

PATRICE *(Running on)*: What's happening?

GIL: It's the return of my looter. He's gone to figure out his next move. We'll be okay.

(Beat.)

PATRICE: I couldn't sleep anyway.

GIL: It's almost time. It'll be morning soon.

PATRICE *(Surprised)*: It's so dark still.

GIL: It gets light all of a sudden.

   (Pause) I'll walk you to the road.

PATRICE: Sometimes, in Georgetown, I stay up through the night. Right through the night. Watching the Potomac. In the dark. And then the first planes starting to come down at National. Jogging congressional aids. Georgetown students who've been up all night, wandering home . . .

(Pause.)

GIL *(Hesitant)*: When did you last see him?

PATRICE: Your father? Ten months ago.

GIL: I imagine he was alone.

PATRICE: There was a girlfriend. Named Goldie. Really. She was sweet. She took care of him. She was a waitress. She did okay. She did enough for the both of them.

 (Beat. She shrugs) We took him out to dinner in Ocean Park, at some Mexican place right before he got sick, and he cried for a minute, but it was really just the margaritas.

GIL: Was there . . . *God forbid* . . . an epiphany before he died?

PATRICE: No. Just that he loved you both very much.

GIL: That's very small beer, isn't it, Mom?

(She nods. There is a moment.)

PATRICE: You know how I got my old job back at The Phillips? I just walked in, and someone actually remembered me. That I had once had "promise." I work with people who are half my age. I like them. They're unafraid. They are fearless . . .

 (Beat) In this light, you look like Alec.

GIL *(Shakes his head)*: Do I? I hope not. He didn't look very . . . the last time I saw him, he—

PATRICE: Tell me. Gil. I have to know.

GIL: You have to name it? You have to be able to see the detail?

PATRICE: I have to name it. Yes.

GIL: You know it was a bullet . . . *(Patrice nods)* . . . to the back of the neck. Behind a grocery store in Soweto. I imagine it was painless. So you don't have to worry about that.

(Beat) I think it was a simple assassination. I was in Kenya with him a few days before, and begged him not to keep going down there. He knew there were many people, with great, vast reasons to kill him. But he kept going anyway. It reached the point where I simply could not stop him. Even Carly couldn't stop him. God knows she stuck it out.

(Beat) He kept going back to South Africa again and again and again. They might have just let him fade away but he wouldn't allow them.

(Beat) And that was that. At least in the end, he got what he wanted.

(Beat) I left Kenya, got to Jo'burg at four in the morning, went to their morgue, and I said "Yes. This is my brother, Alec Dalton Burgess." They gave me his stuff. And I left.

(There is a great, long silence. Neither can speak. Gil turns away.)

PATRICE: If your father could have died in Alec's place, he would have done so without thinking.

GIL: How do you *do* it? How do you get through the *day*, Mom? *Knowing* what you know? Being around people. Because I can't now. I end up in places like this. Look around you. How do you manage to get by, smiling, seeing people, being alive, whatever?

PATRICE: I don't. I'm not. Where I am is as scary as this place, Gil.

(Pause.)

GIL: Have you got your stuff together? If there's a truck . . . You'll have to flag him down. They come by fast. They shoot by and you don't want to miss them. It could be a long wait between rides . . .

(He stops, he's miserable.)

PATRICE: Gil. The way people ask for forgiveness is so meaningless. The little prayers of everyday life. The small print nobody even reads. It's not even part of my language anymore. I eradicated it. I watch myself. In small ways, not able to say "I'm sorry." Something happens. I knock over someone's pencil at work or I cut them off crossing the street and I cannot look at them and say "My mistake." I know that if I begin, I'll just . . .

(Beat) There is nothing, at a certain point, that, I would not have done differently.

(Pause. He looks at her. He nods. He thinks for a moment before speaking.)

GIL: That's something. That's a start.

PATRICE: Is it? Gil?— I hope . . .

(There is rustling from the darkness again.)

GIL: Tenemos nada aqui! Go away! There's nothing here!
   (Beat. He looks at Patrice) Could you maybe just shout
   a little?

PATRICE: Shout?

GIL: So he knows it's not just me. He knows me. I don't scare
   him.
   (Yells) Just give up, can't you.

PATRICE: All right. *(Tentative)* Go away!

GIL: We don't have anything!

PATRICE *(Reluctant, out into the darkness)*: I swear to God, you'd
   better get out of here if you know what's good for you.

GIL *(Smiling)*: Can't you do a little better than that, Patrice?
   You used to be the scariest white woman in Africa.
   (Yells) Get out of here!

PATRICE *(Shouts; a great driving rage)*: Listen you people, I swear
   to God, I'm giving you a minute to get out of here and
   then we're coming after you. Did you hear me?
   (Beat) I'm counting! I'm counting to *three!*

GIL *(Laughs, admiring her)*: Oh, that's *good.* I remember that.
   That's scary.

PATRICE *(A roar)*: One!

GIL AND PATRICE: Two!

(Pause.)

PATRICE *(Very softly, looking at Gil)*: Three.
>   *(Beat. Sound of footsteps running off)* It worked. He's
>   gone.

GIL: He'll be back. Tomorrow night. He'll bring his pals.

PATRICE *(Worried for him)*: What'll you do?

>   *(Pause. He looks at her.)*

GIL: Well. We could scare him again.

>   *(Beat.)*

PATRICE: We could. *(She smiles, understanding what he is actually saying)*

GIL: It's getting lighter . . .

PATRICE: Is it?

GIL: . . . daylight . . .

>   *(Gil shrugs—a throw away—sits down by the fire, looks out.*
>   *Patrice sits across the fire from him.*
>   *The lights come up slowly and then fade.)*

END OF PLAY

A FAIR COUNTRY

by Jon Robin Baitz

Having electrified audiences with *The Substance of Fire,* Jon Robin Baitz now presents this dramatic tour de force about a family wrenched apart by betrayal, guilt, madness and murder.

The play opens at an archaeological dig in a remote area of Mexico. As Gil Burgess examines some broken shards of pottery, his mother appears, whom he hasn't seen in years and who warily attempts to pick up the pieces of their ruptured relationship.

They reminisce, and through flashbacks we learn of their past life in South Africa, where Gil's father was a diplomat. Desperate to get his family out of Africa, Gil's father makes a decision, which has devastating and heartbreaking repercussions on his marriage and family.